GW01179606

The best thing about a book on criminal activity is that it's not criminal activity to create one.

Let this dedication be to whomever reads what I've written without doing any such thing as you've read about.

John Gentry

VICTIMS AND PERPETRATORS

Light Verse Judgement on the
Criminally Inclined

AUSTIN MACAULEY PUBLISHERS™

LONDON • CAMBRIDGE • NEW YORK • SHARJAH

Copyright © John Gentry 2024

All rights reserved. No part of this publication may be reproduced, distributed, or transmitted in any form or by any means, including photocopying, recording, or other electronic or mechanical methods, without the prior written permission of the publisher, except in the case of brief quotations embodied in critical reviews and certain other non-commercial uses permitted by copyright law. For permission requests, write to the publisher.

Any person who commits any unauthorized act in relation to this publication may be liable to criminal prosecution and civil claims for damages.

Ordering Information
Quantity sales: Special discounts are available on quantity purchases by corporations, associations, and others. For details, contact the publisher at the address below.

Publisher's Cataloging-in-Publication data
Gentry, John
Victims and Perpetrators

ISBN 9798886934595 (Paperback)
ISBN 9798886934601 (Hardback)
ISBN 9798886934625 (ePub e-book)
ISBN 9798886934618 (Audiobook)

Library of Congress Control Number: 2023921083

www.austinmacauley.com/us

First Published 2024
Austin Macauley Publishers LLC
40 Wall Street, 3rd Floor, Suite 3302
New York, NY 10005
USA

mail-usa@austinmacauley.com
+1 (646) 5125767

Table of Contents

This is a story.
Someone will say, 'No it's not. It's a bunch of poems.'
Why can't a poem be a story?
A story takes longer.
A longer poem could be a shorter story. Just because it rhymes, it doesn't take away from it being a story as well as a poem.
Poems don't rhyme anymore.
Mine do.
Who ever heard of a story that rhymes?
My stories rhyme because they're also poems.

Turn the page.

Wanted!

Be on the lookout for Leroy.
From city to city he flits,
Where nefarious capers he pulls
And then, very hurriedly, splits.

He whacked a stoolie in Stockton,
Then burgled a Houston Hotel.
He's under suspicion for arson
By the cops in Kalispell.

His credit is lousy in Lubbock.
He's known as a gangster in Gary.
There's a man with a shotgun in Shiloh
Whose daughter he neglected to marry.

He wore out his welcome in Waco,
And departed in haste from Des Moines,
Where he got a job as a teller,
Making off with the cash and the coin.

He cleaned out a bank in Burbank,
After running a red light in Redding.
If they pull him over in Pullman,
It's 20 to life he'll be getting

He is also wanted in our town;
The mayor has formed a committee.
They're looking all over to find him
And award him the key to the city.

Criminal Migrations

Where Batman dwells and Superman
Crime's at a minimum.
Their cities are safe from hooligans;
No crook would be so dumb

As to heist a Gotham City bank
Or Metropolis jewelry store.
With Clark and Bruce both on the job,
Such crimes there are no more.

Lex Luther, the Joker, the portly Penguin
Have all been put to rout,
Their evil henchmen rounded up
And ruthlessly cast out.

You'd think that Superman would then
Go find some other place
To vanquish its corruption and
Make glad its populace.

But the man from Krypton has no plans,
I hear, to pull up stakes
And fly away to Philly and solve
Their criminal headaches.

No Californian has ever looked up
To see him whooshing down
To hold together a bursting dam
And save a threatened town.

A bank holdup in Albany
Batman could easily thwart,
And jewel thieves rifling Tiffany's
No doubt he would abort.

And how would it look for law and order
If the Joker, some dark day,
Makes bail in Gotham City
And moves out to L.A.?

Or what if the Penguin and his pals
Migrate up to Seattle,
Or someplace in Wyoming
And rustle all their cattle?

Such geniuses of crime are far
Beyond the brawn and brain
Of ordinary law enforcement
To outwit and constrain.

Lex Luther is the biggest worry,
The cleverest of the three.
Most likely, he'll head for Washington
And steal the presidency.

He won't be the first crooked president;
There were others before, no doubt.
What a surprise when he finds Fort Knox
Has already been cleaned out!

Hard Rock, Idaho

Way out west off the main highway
There's a place where you don't want to go,
Where mercy is lame and it goes by the name
Of Hard Rock, Idaho.

I was thumbing my way out of Winnemucca
On 95, heading north,
When around the bend, a logging truck
Rattles and rumbles forth.

I waved and caught the trucker's eye
And his rig pulls over to the side;
Down rolls a window and he hollers out loud,
"Hey, Bo, are you lookin' for a ride?"

Well, quicker than you can say, Peterbilt,
I was up in that logging truck,
Motoring north in the heat of the day,
My first real turn of luck.

His radio was playing bluegrass low
As we chatted and laughed and joked,
And I counted the miles as I breathed in the air
Of the stogie that he smoked.

A couple of hours went by and then
The trucker (His name was Wade.)
Says, "Just up the road, I'm turning east
On the Seven Devils' Grade,

And I'm sorry to say, when we separate,
That I've done you no favor, Bo:
When you step down, you'll be in the town
Of Hard Rock, Idaho.

Head straight on through; don't stop for nothin'
For rest or grub or news.
'Cause they'll haul you in for a cross-eyed look,
And don't even think about booze."

Well, I thanked the trucker and waved him on,
And hoisted up my gear
And started down through the center of town,
Of trouble I had no fear.

A sign said: *90 miles to Weiser*
Where a job was waiting for me,
Driving a D12 Caterpillar,
Which was my specialty.

But I was hungry and 90 miles
Was quite a ways to go,
And I clean forgot Wade's caveat
About Hard Rock, Idaho.

I looked around and across the street
Was the Hard Rock Bar & Grill.
So in I went and I liked the place.
Sometime in there I'd kill.

I ordered a big cheese burger with a mess o' fries
And washed it down with a beer,
Played a little country on an old juke box
And sucked up the atmosphere.

The bill it came; it wasn't much
And I scooted back my chair,
And reached for my left hip pocket, but dang!
My wallet wasn't there.

I padded my Levis up and down,
As hope began to fade.
My wallet was gone and on its way
Up the Seven Devils' Grade.

And the trucker's words came back to me,
"Whatever you do now, Bo.
Keep a moving on 'cause you don't wanna hang
In Hard Rock, Idaho."

Then the sheriff came with his big ol' gun
And he says to me, "Son, let's go.
Dead beats we do not tolerate
In Hard Rock, Idaho.

"Just down the street, the local judge
Is waiting to try your case.
He don't take kindly to moochin' bums,
And he happens to own this place

"Where you wolfed down a burger and fries
Without no means to pay.
You'll work it off on the chain-gang
At 50 cents a day.

"Out to the county correctional farm
For 90 days you'll go.
And that's what we call leniency
In Hard Rock, Idaho."

Then he slapped a pair of cuffs on me,
And I was frog-marched out
To where there was an angry mob,
And there seemed little doubt

The milk of human kindness had
Turned sour in that town.
At urban incivility they wore
The undisputed crown

A little ol' lady with a Pekinese
Was wavin' a piece of rope
In which there was a hangman's knot.
Which gave me little hope

That I'd ever make it up to Weiser
Where I could earn some dough,
But would end my days hanging from a limb
In Hard Rock, Idaho.

The women, the children, even the dogs
Were deaf to my appeals.
Their Pitbulls and Rottweilers came,
A snappin' at my heels.

How little that morning in Winnemucca
Did I realize
The penance I would have to pay
For a burger and some fries.

No such vittles ever got served
While I was prisoner there;
Stale bread and bacon lard
And gristle was my fare.

But three days later by the side of the road,
I was hoeing weeds in the sun,
When around the bend comes a logging truck.
"Wade, you son-of-a-gun!"

My wallet he hands me out the window
And says as he steps down,
"I've had a little chat with the local judge,
And they're taking you back to town

"Where you can pay for your burger and fries.
Mooching he still hates.
But he happens to own a construction company
In Weiser where a D12 waits

"For a driver who's coming from Winnemucca,
He's supposed to be pretty good,
But a little careless with his wallet,
Not minding it like he should.

"So get your tail in that black and white
Coming up behind me, Bo.
It's the deputy sheriff, and he's driving you
To Weiser, Idaho."

So, friend, if you're ever on 95 North,
Remember this tale of woe.
And come what may, stay far away from
Hard Rock, Idaho.

The Alibi

So you're a cop. Well, ain't that sweet?
Whadda ya want with me?
Where was I at 2 a.m.?
I ain't done nothin', see.

If you're trying to hang on me some rap,
I got an alibi,
Me and couple of other dudes
Were havin' a pizza pie

From one 'til 3 a.m. at Ruby's
On 14th Avenue.
They told me their names, but I forgot.
They was just passing through.

Coulda been Jones, the bigger one.
The other one, maybe... Smith?
Neither one, the type that I
Would hang around much with.

So, someone swiped the tires off
The squad car of a cop,
While he was busy investigating
Harry's Donut Shop?

What a stinkin' shame dat was.
Hey! Call da FBI.
The streets, they just ain't safe no more.
I think I'm gonna cry!

Yeah, the midnight auto mart
Was once my bailiwick.
I'd cop some hubs and the lock of a trunk
Now and then I'd pick.

But I don't do that stuff no more.
Ask anyone on the street.
The 18 months in the slammer I did,
I wish not to repeat.

You got the wrong guy here; I'm clean.
Your suspicions of me are balmy.
I'm in the clear.
You can't prove nothin'
And besides, nobody saw me.

British Murder Mystery

An invalid she'd been these many years,
The Lady Crutchington, so frail and thin.
Her oldest nephew, Winston, was her heir,
In frightful debt to quite unscrupulous men.

But all that changed one dismal rainy morn
When they went in and found that she had croaked.
There were some purple marks upon her neck,
But they quashed the nasty rumor she'd been choked.

And hardly had the body been removed
Then Winston poked around to find her will,
And what he read soon put his mind at rest,
But the deadly hand of fate would cast a chill

When they found him on the iron picket fence,
Impaled from having fallen from the roof.
Which proved to the advantage of his brothers,
A pair to whom he'd always been aloof.

Ten thousand British sterling pounds apiece
Both Reginald and Nigel stood to gain,
But hardly was poor Winston laid to rest
Then Nigel took two bullets to the brain.

They found the lethal weapon by his head--
A British Webley-Vickers .303,
And in what Reggie said was Nigel's hand,
A note explaining his 'despondency.'

Even though for years they'd seldom spoken,
Reginald was shaken to the core,
Sadly grieving o'er his brother's loss,
Though richer for it by 10,000 more.

So, "What a pity!" they all said when Reg,
Two days later tripped and headlong fell,
By accident with no one else around,
To the bottom of an old, abandoned well.

Now who'd gain those unclaimed sterling pounds?
It soon fell out that all of it must go
To a cousin, twice removed, from Liverpool,
The Duchess of the Duke of Rochambeau.

But hardly had she moved her baggage in
And proved herself of legal ancestry,
Then she went into convulsions and she died
From something disagreeable in her tea.

Now who was next in line to benefit?
It soon was clear the butler, Jeeves, would be,
Because of all the others' sad demise,
Lady Crutchington's new beneficiary.

But when they pulled the butler cord for Jeeves,
The upstairs maid, Miss Betty Bligh, rushed in
Announcing very mournfully that she
Had sadly found the butler's head crushed in.

Then dutifully excused herself to find
The gardener who'd not heard of this mishap,
Nor the news that he was now the lucky heir,
But he'd accidentally hanged himself. Poor chap!

The handyman, Montgomery, they now sought
To tell him of the sterling pounds he'd earned.
But a corpse was all he was when he was found
In the ashes of the furnace where he'd burned.

So, on and on the tragedy unfolded
And one by one the others met their fate,
Until no one was left but Betty Bligh,
The upstairs maid, with whom I have a date.

The Dame at the
Sands Motel

It's 2 a.m. and I'm bruised and sore;
The night is rainy and cold.
They've thrown a dragnet out for me,
And they'll shoot to kill, I'm told.

A chopper hovers overhead,
Its searchlight glowers down,
Sweeping to and fro to find
And run me to the ground.

I'm out of cash, been out of food
For two days, maybe three,
And 'wanted' posters are everywhere
With a big reward for me.

They've found by now my gassed-out wreck,
Its engine blown to hell,
And the key to the room where lying dead
Is a dame at the Sands Motel.

In a pool of blood they'll find a gun
That's registered to me,
And they're going to say I shot her dead
In a fit of jealousy.

Hot on my trail is a driven man,
Single-minded, I'll attest;
In the pocket behind his sheriff's badge
Is a warrant for my arrest.

He'd rather shoot than read my rights,
Of that I'm satisfied.
He's on the take, that rotten cop!
He's double-crossed and lied,

And he knows that I am on to him,
And he's laid for me a trap,
That for that body at the Sands Motel
I should take the rap.

That's why I'm on the lam right now,
And the cold wind's like a knife.
I'm looking hard at a prison term
For the rest of my natural life.

There's a freight coming through at 4:15,
Headed north and out of town,
And I'll catch a ride in an open car
At the bend where it always slows down.

I can hear the train whistle on the cold night wind
As it rumbles along the track,
Moving slow like an iron ghost
With an eerie *clickety-clack*.

I'm a dead man running—a passenger,
On the 4:15 to hell.
But hell's where I'll find the man who murdered
The dame at the Sands Motel.

An empty box car rumbles by,
And I leap for the open door
And crack my head on a wooden pallet
As I roll across the floor.

I'm in one piece, but I'm seeing stars,
Then voices fill the air
With a soft piano, a clink of glasses
And the wooden scrape of chair.

Where am I? The rumbling freight,
Where did everything go?
I'm in a bar with a drink in my hand.
I'm reeling to and fro.

Then something wet runs down my forehead,
And sticky. I think it's blood.
The drink slips out of my hand. I stagger.
My brain has turned to mud.

Cymbals clash from a symphony,
Cocoa nuts fall from a tree.
A hyena laughs, and I wish someone
Would finish this poem for me.

Bad Ideas

I'd hitch a ride up north to Juneau,
And maybe jack a truck, you know,
But that's a bad idea.

I'd find a busy street and range
Up and down and pan for change,
But that's a bad idea.

I'd scrounge through empties in a dumpster bin
For maybe a drop or two of gin,
But that's a bad idea.

I'd paw through brass spittoons and sort
For butts and stogies, not too short,
But that's a bad idea.

I'd heist an all-night liquor store
And blow the money on a whore,
But that's a bad idea.

I'd find a dealer I used to know
And weasel half an ounce of snow,
But that's a bad idea.

I'd find a backwoods country bar
And drink white lightning from a jar,
But that's a bad idea.

I'd find a wino, tanked and prone,
And pick his pockets to the bone,
But that's a bad idea.

I'd take a hot bath, slit a vein
And let it all run down the drain,
But that's a bad idea.

I'd sober up and wash and shave,
And maybe, after that, behave.
NAH!

The L.A. County Jail

In the county slammer (which is a jail)
And impecunious towards my bail,
I met this dude from the cell next door,
Prisoner three-five-six-nine-four,
Who said he'd teach me day by day,
How I might profit from my stay
At the L.A. County Jail.

His moniker was Felony Fred,
Who, with his arm around me, said,
It'd been some time since he was out
But still he was, without a doubt,
The king of crime beyond dispute
At the West Coast Criminal Institute,
The L.A. County Jail.

He asked if I would take the time
To learn the arts and crafts of crime.
Which I would do, no sweat, for sure
And soon became a connoisseur.
At cons I passed up all the others
And larceny with flying colors
At the L.A. County Jail.

For fame and fortune, I had a plan,
And when no longer in the can,
I'd go all out to fleece the sheep,
And learn to clip them in my sleep.
A reputation I quickly earned
From all the foibles I had learned
At the L.A. County Jail.

Branching out soon after that,
At forgery, I went to bat.
Signatures I penned so fine
Of loaded dudes, which was a sign
My talents had begun to gel,
And I had learned my lessons well
At the L.A. County Jail.

A partnership in crime then we
Formed, a classy dame and me.
We ran a scam most reprobate,
In big-time corporate real estate
She knew a thing or two on crime,
Cause just like me she'd spent some time
At the L.A. County Jail.

One last job, she said one day,
Would for the both of us defray
All our criminal wants and wishes
Leaving us the most delicious
Pile of gilded stocks and bonds
Far away from the locked-up cons
At the L.A. County Jail.

The big payoff would come when Sam
(The mark we'd picked to flim and flam)
Inked his name to some shady stuff.
Meaning that him, right by the scruff
We had, but then popped up some gents
With badges saying they represent
The L.A. County Jail.

A pair of cuffs they slapped on me
With hints that jail time there'd be.
The judge was stern, the trial swift.
With juries that D.A. had a gift.
My new career awaits, they said,
As Jr. partner to Felony Fred
At the L.A. County Jail.

But that's not all; there's one thing more,
That classy dame I mentioned before,
That mistress of the perfect fleece,
She was herself of the police!
But no less classy, and daily I eye
Her through the bars as she walks by
The L.A. County Jail.

Bank Job

Nervous Norman was robbing a bank.
He'd never done it before.
With a Smith & Wesson and an empty bag
He waited 'til quarter past four.

Then said to the teller in a voice he thought
Conveyed his derring-do,
"Put all your cash inside this gun;
I'm holding a bag on you."

Biker Dudes

At Zoey's back in 98,
They let me up on stage.
To read a poem at the open mic
Back then was quite the rage.

My piece was on the biker's life:
And how he spent his days,
His ridin' and his drinkin' and
His wild and reckless ways.

Well, I'd hardly read the first three lines
Then I raised my eyes and saw
The whole front row was biker dudes,
Red-eyed, mean, and raw.

Their leader looked like a mutant from
Rod Sterling's Twilight Zone.
The scar that ran from his hairline down
Was red clean to the bone,

The dude behind him seemed to smile,
His teeth was showing white.
But later, they told me it was what'd been done
With a tire chain one night.

Another cuss wore leather pants,
His head shaved to the skin,
Pierced with studs at his ears and lips
With a scraggly beard on his chin.

And they were the cleanest cut of the lot,
The rest were a whole lot worse:
Bruised and scarred by the savagery
Of the outlaw bikers' curse.

Well, I finished my poem on a biker's life;
I thought I'd done my best.
The applause was tepid, but I could see
The bikers weren't impressed.

Then, without a word, they all stood up,
With looks like homicide,
And surrounded me as their leader announced:
"We're takin' you for a ride."

And before I knew it, I was hustled out
To a row of Harley's in back.
About a biker's life, they said,
This poet didn't know Jack.

Like a sack of spuds, they threw me on
A hog behind the dude
That had the permanent chain-made smile
And he didn't seem in the mood

To take me for a granny cruise
So I held on like grim death
As his rear wheel made a ripping spin
That took away my breath.

The noise was like the crack of doom,
The gravel flew nine yards,
And I knew that a quiet, joy ride
Just wasn't in the cards.

Like a maddened steed that bike reared up
In a wheelie of 40 degrees,
Then roared down the alley with me hangin' on
And tremblin' at the knees.

Then all the other bikers followed,
Like wild horses on the run,
Over the bridge at the foot of Main
And on to the 101.

North we sped—a motorized herd
Of hell-bent outlaw dudes,
A howlin' bunch of brass-knuckle bikers,
A pack of attitudes.

How long we roared through the starry night
Along the Rincon Coast,
With me a hangin' on for life
To the back of my biker host,

I can't remember and it's best I don't,
It would only stoke my fear,
But I do recall a beach campfire,
Cookin' and a river of beer.

Then after that, we were back on the road,
Doin' 80 all the way to town,
And up the alley back of Zoey's Café,
Where they roughly set me down.

The biker boss, I guess, assumed
That Zoey's was my home.
"You're lucky," he said. "By a margin of one,
We voted thumbs-up on your poem."

Business Opportunities

Business opportunities,
There have never been so many.
Prospects abound in our town
If you're looking around for any.

The possibilities are rife
For business after dark;
You can partner with the muggers
Or the druggies in the park.

Just south of Main, across the tracks,
The poker parlors thrive.
One block from there, when darkness falls,
The strip joints come alive.

The porno shops on Sycamore
Are where the weirdos hang
To hustle change and peddle crack
And passersby harangue.

The tattoo parlor trade is brisk,
The piercings and the studs
Bring differentiations to
The Homies and the Bloods.

Our liquor stores are fully stocked,
So busy is their trade,
You can also lay an off-track bet,
Except when there's a raid.

The walkup hotel rooms are cheap
At 40 bucks an hour,
Companionship included, but
It's extra for a shower.

There are loan sharks just across the street,
Where you might muscle in.
Tardy payments are no problem
With a whack across the shin.

So that's the business climate here
In our community.
From market ups and downs we offer
No immunity.

Great perseverance it takes to be
An entrepreneurial hero,
For a fee, there are endorsements from
Our Better Business Bureau.

Criminal City

I'm the king of Criminal City,
The big enchilada of crime.
When I want a piece of the action, move over
'Cuz I operate big time.

I own the mayor and the city council,
And I keep 'em all in line.
The chief of police don't give me no trouble;
The pimps and hookers are mine.

The city aldermen answer to me;
They're all on my payroll,
And my spies in the press manipulate
The public opinion poll.

I run the numbers and I lay the odds
For the bookies at the track,
And I take my share of the house proceeds
From bingo and black jack.

I run a protection service and squeeze
Them legit business chumps.
Ten percent of their profits I rake,
Or my goons make wit da lumps.

But it's been a while since I made any dough,
And my profits have taken a hit.
There's hardly anyone left to chisel,
'Cuz da honest folks have split.

The Dark Side of the Moon

(Revising Pink Floyd)

On the dark side of the moonshine still,
Is where I hid from the feds with Bill.

Them revenuers pulled up in cars
And busted up our moonshine jars,

But me and Bill they did not catch.
Next week, we'll make another batch.

Family Values

My sister was a psycho; my brother peddled drugs.
Talk smack to my ol' man and he would fill you full of
slugs.

Mama was a porno queen and a kleptomaniac.
My uncle ran a crap game and the numbers at the track.

My nephew's in San Quentin on a grand theft auto
charge,
But later slipped a chain gang and is presently at large.

They're looking for my brother-in-law for passing bogus
bills,
And distilling moonshine whiskey in the Santa Ana hills.

A second cousin's on trial for an arson fire he set.
They caught him twice before; 20 years he'll get.

It's lonely at reunions—there's no one there but me.
The rest are on the lam or under lock and key.

But far away am I from being the family pride & joy,
'Cause I threw away tradition and became a choir boy.

Hoodlums' Christmas

Charlie was a thug, a crook,
Until one Christmas, the spirit took
His soul and somehow softened it,
More than just a little bit.

And Charlie, thereafter, had a heart of gold,
And it was his endeavor to remove from the cold
The down and out and the out of luck
By dunning passersby for a charity buck.

At which Big Charlie was unsurpassed,
Homeless himself way back in the past.
His street pitch was crude but delivered with dash
And never once failed to rake in the cash.

One day on the street, I overhear
His spiel to a well-suited dude passing near.
Taking on an expression both doleful and grim,
This is what he says to him:

"Friend, I see by the cut of your clothes,
That you are a citizen who very well knows
The ins and the outs of how fortunes are made,
And for my shabby lot you'd not likely trade.

"You have friends in high places where I have none;
You have club memberships and a place in the sun.
You can travel abroad and are loaded with dough
And frequent posh places where I cannot go.

"On the other hand, I have some privileges, too
With muscle-bound guys in low places who,
According to stories, I was told in the slammer
Are very adroit with blackjack and hammer.

"Yes, low-level friends in low-level places,
Insensitive gorillas who rearrange faces,
Or break a few bones when it's deemed necessary,
Like my cousin, Vinnie, and his big brother, Harry.

"They frequent low places where they go by nicknames:
Like Chainsaw Chuck and Jawbreaker James,
Two goons that you certainly would not want to meet
In a dim-lighted alley or on a dark street.

"And such are the upstanding citizens that,
At my suggestion would take a ball bat
To a homeless guy or a cripple ol' lady,
And such other deeds that are crooked and shady.

"But that need not be in your case, my friend.
My hustling of you has a much nobler end.
Ordinarily, I take action as a lawless galoot,
But I'm ringing this bell in a Santa Clause suit

"In order to fill up this pot you see here
With dough to dump some Christmas cheer
On that cripple ol' lady I mentioned before,
And the homeless guy to open the door

"To a warm bowl of soup and a bed for the night,
For which they have not makes me very uptight,
And gives me the urge to dial up and tweet
Vinnie and Harry from across the street.

"Harry is a reindeer and Vinnie's an elf.
Their suits are adorable; I made them myself.
They would like nothing better than accosting and whacking
Some tightfisted citizen whose charity was lacking.

"A voluntary financial transaction,
I suggest, is much better than three weeks in traction.
A clatter of coinage and big bills I hear.
Very generous! Thank you, and Happy New Year!"

Hopeless Case

Her trial begins this morning at nine.
It's dawn now at half past five.
A prominent citizen lies dead, and my client
Was the last one to see him alive.

There are witnesses against her who swear they were there
When she threatened to blow him away.
He had two-timed her, cheated, and lied, she said,
And the rat was going to pay.

Three bullets they found in his chest from a gun
With her fingerprints on the grip.
For the time of the crime, she has no alibi;
And she says she doesn't give a rip.

My opening argument is full of holes;
The D.A. will tear it apart.
And the newspaper guys have screamed on Page One,
"She's guilty," right from the start.

And the judge is against me; he has an old score,
I once took him to school on a case.
I made him look bad in front of a jury,
And I mocked him to his face.

He'd scuttle my case in a New York minute
Just to even the score,
And maybe pull strings so I couldn't practice
Before the bar anymore.

But no matter how hopeless, I'm still gonna win,
'Cause I have a silent partner:
I'm Perry Mason and my ace in the hole
Is Erle Stanley Gardner.

I Bought a Hat in Tehachapi

I bought a hat in Tehachapi
At the Good Luck Second-Hand Store.
A soft, brown, felt fedora-three bucks.
The tax was a little bit more.

A good luck bargain at a Good Luck Store,
I walked out wearing a smile.
Maybe good fortune will come along with it
And follow me around for a while.

Just outside, I took the hat
And stuck it on my head,
Got into my car and turned the key,
But the battery was dead.

No problemo. Down at the corner
There stood a Chevron sign.
I'd push on down and get a charge
Then everything'd be fine.

Just then, a tall, blue-suited man
With a shiny badge and a stick
Informed me that the parking space
That I just happened to pick

Was painted red along the curb
Which was to indicate
Violators will be towed,
Then wrote down my license plate.

Following that, with a wave of his hand,
There suddenly appeared,
From around the corner, the city wrecker,
Which was just as I feared.

I bought the car that afternoon
From an acned, pothead youth,
Stoned to the gills in a tie-dye shirt,
And that's the honest truth.

For miscellaneous weed and such,
He might have left behind,
I started on a thorough search,
But then thought, *Never mind.*

I'll browse around the thrift store first,
And give it a shakedown later.
But the kid in the ways of pot turned out
To be no second-rater.

A pack of Zigzags was on the floor,
And I thought they'd let that pass,
But in the cushions they discovered
A hiding place for grass.

Underneath the seat, they found
Three roach clips and some ludes,
And in the trunk, a hookah pipe
For the really kinky dudes.

And from a plastic first aid kit
There fell out on the ground,
Little tiny packets of
What looked like Mexican brown.

Two hours later in Tehachapi,
With my license invalidated,
Both me and my crack-head, towed-away car
Had been incarcerated.

Soon after that I was arraigned,
Mug-shot and fingerprinted,
And prospects of a prison term
Was very strongly hinted.

Later at the holding cell,
In my big orange prisoner suit,
That hat seemed about as lucky for me
As a cement parachute.

But the very next day in Tehachapi,
The sheriff set me free.
No explanation, just: "Get outta town!"
It seemed a mystery.

From sending me up for 20 years
I thought they'd never budge;
But the pothead kid who sold me the car,
His ol' man was the judge!

Legal Proceedings

The witness on the witness stand
Was addled, confused and crazed.
The deep and probing examination,
Unanswered questions raised:

Who found the body? Where is the gun?
Who is missing a glove?
How had the murderer entered the room?
Was the motive envy or love.

Were there signs of a struggle? Was robbery the aim?
Could the assailant have been a friend?
Could blackmail possibly have been involved?
Just who would gain in the end?

As all the pieces came together,
The jurors were amazed,
And Perry Mason's brilliant cross
Left Mr. Berger dazed.

Leroy and Caesar

(An L.A. gangland version of Percy French's 1877 poem,
Abdul Abulbul Amir)

The boys of the hood were daring and bold
And quite unaccustomed to fear,
But the bravest by far in the ranks of the bloods
Was Leroy Roosevelt Greer.

If you wanted some cat in a daredevil mood
To shoplift a six-pack of beer,
Or ale or stout, you had only to shout
For Leroy Roosevelt Greer.

In the barrios, they know and the Homies all go
For duck tails and custom-built cars,
And the most so inclined to the low-rider line
Was Caesar Jesus Escovar.

He could mix margaritas, breakdance, and tango
And strum on his homey guitar.
In fact quite the cream of the barrio team
Was Caesar Jesus Escovar.

One day, this Latino in his fine tailored threads,
And wearing a truculent sneer,
Did drive his Gran Prix to the gang territory
Of Leroy Roosevelt Greer.

"Now, dude," said Leroy, "if you've came to destroy
Or otherwise snuff my career,
You must make your debut with the steel razoo
Of Leroy Roosevelt Greer.

"So take your last gaze at the turf and the haze.
Say goodbye to your low-rider car,
And know, I intend to make a swift end
Of Caesar Jesus Escovar."

Then a grimace he made as he whipped out the blade
To whittle a permanent scar,
And with murderous intent, he ferociously went
For Caesar Jesus Escovar.

Then Caesar he parried with the knife that he carried,
A six-inch stiletto, spring-loaded.
Then flailed away, those two, until they
From head to toe were blood-coated.

They fought all that day and into the night,
The din it was heard from afar.
As multitudes came, so great was the fame
Of Greer and Escovar.

As Escovar's knife was extracting his life,
Leroy's blood splattered far,
As his razor did drain the jugular vein
Of Caesar Jesus Escovar.

The bloods from the hood, they whooped where they
stood
Their hero they thought they would cheer,
But only drew nigh to hear the last sigh
Of Leroy Roosevelt Greer

On a stone o'er a grave in south central L.A.
And carved in characters clear
You can read of the duel that brought on the cruel
Demise of Roosevelt Greer.

And a Latina maiden her lone vigil keeps
In the quiet Olvera Street Bar,
And the name that she murmurs in vain as she weeps
Is Caesar Jesus Escovar.

The Liars' Club

"TO THE LIARS' CLUB." That's all it said,
A small painted sign in the alley, which Fred

Had never noticed before, until
He happened to stray, as pedestrians will,

From his usual morning walk downtown,
Through a narrow alleyway he had found.

And just beneath the sign, a door,
Which looked like it hadn't been opened before

And Fred thought, *No use trying that,*
And pulled down the brim of his brown felt hat

To turn away from the curious door.
But something moved him to turn once more

Toward the Liars' Club sign, in case
It turned out to be some business place,

Or better yet, a social club
For cocktails and convivial hub-bub.

With this in mind, the door he tried,
And to his surprise, it opened wide

Revealing steps leading up and around,
Carpeted green to muffle the sound

Of his footsteps on the silent stairs.
Foolishness, he thought. *Who cares?*

What kind of a club would stigmatize
Itself with such a name? Unwise

It seemed, to say the least, but still
Something drew him against his will

To, step by step, continue his tread
Upward where the stairway led.

He came to a landing, but there wasn't a door
That opened out to the second floor

As one might expect, so up and around
He climbed until at last he found.

Another sign that read: *This Way*
To the Liars' Club—Open All Day.

And where the sign pointed, he hurriedly went
Pursuing his 'Liars' Club' enlightenment.

And on a large door at the end of the hall,
In very wide letters, italic and tall,

The Liars' Club. Please come in.
And Fred, he did so with a grin

Which turned to horror a moment later
As down he plunged where the elevator

Used to be, but no longer ran,
Making Fred at the bottom a wiser man

With the certain knowledge, as his life expires,
That liars' club signs are made by liars.

The Lyin' King

He was the king, the lyin' king;
He was the king of lies.
Prevarication was his game,
But let me summarize:

He lied to the press, he lied to the people,
He lied to the cop on the beat.
He lied to the bailiff, he lied to the judge.
He lied to the man in the street.

He lied about me and where I was
When the bank got robbed that night.
He lied under oath, he lied to the jury.
His lies were out of sight.

And with his lies, the truth was buried
And swept beneath the rug.
My lawyer lied to kingdom come,
Which kept me out of the jug.

Lucrezia's Feast

Lucrezia Borgia of Italy, we're told,
Was ruthless, conniving, amoral, and bold.
And all that scheming milieu
Of condottiere that she knew

Were steeped in intrigue of all sorts
Throughout those Machiavellian Courts.
The evil Borgias were much involved,
They say, in murders yet unsolved.

And to this day, it sends a chill,
To contemplate her plot to kill
A cabal of her adversaries
With toxin rendered from nightshade berries.

The belladonna fruit is red,
A warning that you'd soon be dead
If you so much as broke the skin
And sipped the deadly juice within.

Your heart would stop; your throat would seize,
And, gasping purple, you'd fall to your knees
And in a half a minute more,
You'd crumple dead upon the floor.

Love apples they were called back then,
Which, lovers on occasion, when
Rejection of their ardor followed,
In desperation, bit and swallowed.

So choosing death beneath a stone
To unrequited love alone.
And so Lucrezia, with this in mind
Scoured all Italy for just this kind

To feed her foes in a sauce or soup
And curl their toes in one fell swoop.
She'd have it poured on fettuccini
With maybe just a little teeny

Bit of spices, perchance to hide
The poisonous taste before they died.
All was made ready on a fateful night.
The banquet hall was a blaze of light.

The crystal gleamed in the candles' glow.
The napery was white as snow.
The fatal sauce was rich and red,
And soon to all her foes was fed.

Lucrezia waited, impatient for
The first dead guest to hit the floor.
But no one fell. Instead they ate
Every smidgeon on their plate

And asked for more when that was gone.
And so they dined until the dawn.
And not one guest so much as fainted
From all that sauce that she had tainted.

Love apples, indeed, she had mixed in her brew,
But the rumors of poison were rumors untrue.
Much less to the condottiere's loss,
Lucrezia had invented tomato sauce.

Money Talks Too Much

They caught me at the scene with a smoking gun.
I sure enough did the guy in.
Murder One brought life or the gas chamber, maybe
But manslaughter brings only ten.

So if I latched on to a pliable jurist
With a bribe of a hefty ten grand.
And she holds out for a manslaughter finding,
In ten years, I'm a free man.

So I found my patsy, a blond young thing,
Who took the ten-grand bait.
And finally after three weeks holding out,
Ten years, not life, was my fate.

I arranged the payment and thanked her on
A call from my prison cell.
"I owe you my life," I told her with glee.
"Ten years is better than hell."

Getting Murder One reduced like that,
The D.A. must be in a fit.
"Well, it wasn't easy," said the blonde I'd bought.
"All the rest of them wanted to acquit."

Olivia's Garden

Olivia's in her garden.
That's her favorite place,
The loam between her fingers,
The sunshine on her face.

She'd rather plant and putter,
And weed and trim and hoe.
But sometimes I'd get hungry.
I couldn't cook, you know.

I asked her very nicely
If her gardening she would stop
And come inside and fix for me
A porterhouse or chop.

But she adamantly wouldn't
"No," she said, "I'll never.
And that's how things are gonna be
For always and forever."

But since that time, I have acquired
Some culinary powers.
I eat alone while Olivia
Is pushing up her flowers.

The Robber

(After the Highwayman: different era, different
country, with apologies to Alfred Noyes)

A great full moon had risen; a wind was in the trees.
The clouds were heaped in billows, like waves on stormy
seas.
The road was a moonlight ribbon where the farmland
rose and fell,
As the robber drove up in a roadster,
A V-8 Packard Roadster
Drove in and parked his roadster at the Midnight Star
Motel

He sported a brown fedora with a diamond pin through
his tie;
His tailored suit was pinstriped—the finest money
could buy.
The trousers were knife-edged creased, like silk in the
light of the moon.
And he strode with a jaunty swagger,
A carefree, lawless swagger,
A *bonvivant* kind of swagger, as he whistled a ragtime
tune.

The grounds were dark and quiet as he tapped on a
pinewood door,
And pressed his ear to the portal, then paused a minute
more.
"Faye," he called in the moonlight.
"Faye, open up. It's me."
Then he waited alone in the moonlight,

58

With scarcely a breath in the moonlight.
Inside, she woke in the moonlight; and the hour was quarter past three.

She opened the door and trembled as the robber slipped inside.
Six hours he'd driven to meet her weary from the all-night ride.
But he was a felon, hunted, and she was the love of his life.
And he pressed her mouth with kisses,
Covered her eyes with kisses,
Wild, hungry kisses, born of stress and strife.

"One last job," he told her, and said once more with a kiss,
"There's a bank I've cased in Evanston; it's a prize I cannot miss.
The vault stands open all day, and the guards are old and slow.
And it's all mine for the taking,
The bonds and the cash for the taking,
Then the back roads I'll be taking, and after that, lie low.

I'll come for you on the morrow before the noonday sun.
But if they're close behind me,
I'll wait till the day is done.
They'll scour the county to catch me, but the odds of that are small.
Then look for me by moonlight,
Watch for me by moonlight,
I'll come for you by moonlight. To hell with the Feds and all."

In the dark outside her window, where the sash was,
raised a crack,
There stood in the shadows listening, the motel
grounds man, Jack.
He burned with a jealous rage, his eyes were rimmed in
red,
As he heard them love in the darkness
And he vowed revenge in the darkness,
Then stole away in the darkness, remembering the
words they said.

He did not come at noontime; the road lay bare all day.
But down the lane at evening, a bloodhound's mournful
bay,
Then a rumble of engines she heard, coming over the
rise of the land.
A cavalcade of troopers,
Uniformed state troopers,
Armed and grim-faced troopers, with loaded guns in
hand.

They were less than gentle with Faye and cuffed her at
the scene.
And bound one hand to a pipe at the back of the ice
machine.
She could see the empty roadway through the slowly
gathering fog.
The posse was armed and hidden,
Hidden along the roadway,
Hidden to ambush her lover and gun him down like a dog

Her fettered wrist was reddened, chafed by the steel
ring.
But she would not count the cost, in spite of the pain it
would bring,
And twisted and pulled at the iron, biting her tongue at
the pain.
Til her slender hand was broken,
Broken and streaked with blood,
Broken but free of the shackle at the first hard drops
of rain.

There was death in the waiting shadows.
Somehow, he had to be told.
Then the distant drone of an engine, she heard through
the rain and the cold.
As dark, up the country roadway, with the lights out,
moving slow,
Came a V-8 Packard Roadster,
Under the guns came the roadster,
And they set dead aim on the roadster as the cold rain
turned to snow.

A desperate plan came to her as she ran through the
freezing rain,
To a lone squad car in the trees and ignoring the
tearing pain,
She groped in the dark on the dashboard for the
switch to the warning red light
He was less than a mile when he saw it,
Like an angry red eye when he saw it,
And he turned the wheel when he saw it and sped off
into the night.

Then all eyes turned on Faye, with her broken hand clutched to her side.
She stood like a prey to the lions, cornered with nowhere to hide.
Then bolted like a deer for the darkness, as a rifle cracked in the air.
Striking her down on the roadway,
Dead through the heart on the roadway,
Where she lay on her face in the roadway, with the wind and the rain in her hair.

It was not til the dawn he heard it, and it fell like a hammer blow,
How bravely she'd tried to warn him and died in the rain and the snow.
He gunned with a vengeance his engine and roared down the rutted lane.
Shrieking a madman's curse,
A curse on the cops and the feds,
A curse for the death of his Faye, for his love lying dead in the rain.

There were 34 holes in the windshield and 159 more
Had riddled the Packard Roadster through the engine, the tires, and the door.
Twenty-one holes had the pinstriped suit (the finest that money could buy),
When they shot him down on the roadway,
Down like a dog on the roadway,
Where he lay in his blood on the roadway, with a diamond pin through his tie.

And still they say of a stormy night, when the wind is in the trees,
And the clouds are heaped in billows like waves on stormy seas,
And the road is a moonlight ribbon where the farmlands rise and fall,
A man drives up in a roadster,
A V-8 Packard Roadster,
Turns in and parks his roadster to make a late-night call.

Up the pathway he strides and stops at a pinewood door,
And softly taps at the portal, then listens a minute more. "Faye," he calls in the moonlight.
"Faye, open up. It's me."
Alone he waits in the moonlight,
With scarcely a breath in the moonlight,
Then she opens the door in the moonlight, and the hour is quarter past three.

The Ballad of Wilma Sue

I did my share of drinkin' when
A younger man I was
Glasses quite a few I'd hoist
'Fore I'd even get a buzz.

Which all came to a screechin' halt
Way back in '92
It was a woman who changed my ways,
And her name was Wilma Sue.

I met her at the south of Tulsa
In a backwoods country bar,
Where all the rednecks came to drink
White lightning from a jar.

They'd made a bar bet—her and the boys,
On who'd be standin' last.
By nine-fifteen, all seven men
Were hopelessly outclassed.

Go swapping shots with Wilma Sue
And you were sure to lose.
Hard drinkers east and west all knew
She was the queen of booze.

It's hard to think of anything
That woman couldn't do.
Prodigious were the mighty deeds
And ways of Wilma Sue

The tattoos on her forearms with her motto:
HAVE NO FEAR,
The skull and crossbones dangling from
Her cauliflower ear

The bar bet that she won the night
She downed three fifths of gin,
The S.W.A.T. team that she busted up
When they tried to take her in.

In every gin mill, east and west,
Where whiskey glasses clink,
They knew the name of Wilma Sue,
Oh, how that gal could drink!

And then one day, she disappeared;
She plumb dropped out of sight.
Could have been her liver went,
Or a bar room brawl one night

Left her broken up and sore
And no one around to care.
Rumor was: she'd ended up
In a pauper's grave somewhere.

Years passed, and then the temperance women
Came in to town one day
To sober up the boys and chase
Ol' Demon Rum away.

On the edge of town in a vacant lot
They pitched their meetin' tent,
And plastered signs up everywhere
Advertising an event

Where the Temperance Arm Wrestling Champ
Was coming in to town
With a rhinestone studded pair o' boots
For whoever takes the crown.

Three big men from Duggin's Pub,
Two more from Millie's Bar
And other drinkers no one knew
Come in from near and far.

And only a couple reconsidered
Their braggadocio
When they learned that them which took a pin
Must on the wagon go.

Well, the weekend came for the big affair
Which filled the meetin' tent
With folks all eager for the wrestlin' match
Which was the main event.

At eight o'clock sharp they opened a flap
Of the big white tent, and there,
Flexing her biceps, was Willma Sue,
With a smile and a bow in her hair.

Ninety-six men she had put on the wagon,
And 14 more that day.
That bar room brawl I mused about,
It happened just that way.

When Wilma tells it, she tells it straight
Her message loud and clear.
And the only thing she's never changed
Is her motto: *HAVE NO FEAR.*

It turned out later that Wilma and me,
As you might well expect,
Just sort o' hit it off in spite
Of the manhood that she wrecked.

Our mutual attraction was
Sincere and bona fide.
But a painful memory kept us apart,
Perhaps it was my pride.

Even though enamored by
Her pugilistic charm,
I was the last of the 14 men,
And she dang near broke my arm.

History Lesson

She was a connoisseur of classics,
A maven of the arts.
At the theater and the opera,
She knew the player's parts.

In every marble-walled museum,
In Washington, D.C.
She was known among the patrons
For her cultured repartee.

At civic restorations, too,
Of famous history sites,
Her elbows rubbed with D.C.'s finest
Luminary lights.

But husband, Fred, not so inclined
To such soiree affairs,
Had tickets to the stadium,
The Redskins and the Bears.

It was his heart's desire to
Attend the game that night
But she had other plans for him
And that stirred up a fight.

Some famous place of history, she
Insisted that he take her.
The football game was down the tubes,
No way that he could make her.

Some famous place from Lincoln's day,
She said would be sublime.
Like a bandstand or a theater
Where Abe had spent some time.

And from that heated altercation
A tragedy ensued,
He'd give her history, sure enough,
But with an attitude.

The irony was spectacular
When something snapped in Fred,
And he took her to Ford's Theater
Where he shot her in the head.

Medieval Melodrama

Wilhelmena longed for love,
And in her mind's eye dreamed
Someday her shining knight would come,
Even though it seemed

The fates were all conspiring
To drive away romance.
The drudgery surrounding her
Offered little chance

That anyone of noble bearing,
Endowed with manly charms,
Would come along and notice her
And take her in his arms.

In bondage, she'd been cheaply sold
To toil for her keep
Under the cruel, penurious eye
Of the duke of Grimsby, the creep.

And to such villainy he was
Inclined, the treacherous cad,
He pressed himself to have his way
Upon the maid. Egad!

Each day, he plotted and connived,
Cajoled her, fumed and cussed
To inveigle Wilhelmena to
Surrender to his lust.

But she steadfastly held him off
With piteous pleas and cries,
Resistant to his blandishments,
Impervious to his lies,

Until his patience at an end,
He clapped her in his dungeon
And threatened her with rack and wheel,
That dastardly curmudgeon!

Meanwhile, not very far afield,
A stranger riding by
Reined in his steed as lo, he heard
A muffled female cry.

A damsel in distress, thought he,
And spurred his mount toward
The screams that came and came again,
As he unsheathed his sword

And hacked to pieces a wooden gate
And rode into the yard
Right past a knave in rusted mail
The duke had put on guard.

Then under the archway and down the steps
He went in rescue mode.
But sometimes things don't always go
The way of chivalry's code.

Wilhelmena, down below
Began to reconsider:
The duke was cruel but rich.
The stranger was poor, the lowest bidder.

And so she made her fateful choice,
And the duke became her man.
But after they were married, that's
When all the change began.

She didn't like his truculence,
His dungeon or his whips.
She told him he must change or no more
Kisses from her lips.

The duke is mild-mannered now.
His cruel sneer is gone.
Instead of the former skull drudgery,
He trims and mows the lawn.

The dungeon is hung with curtains of lace,
The walls with tapestry.
Where Lady Grimsby's club convenes
At three o'clock for tea.

Drinkin' Buddies

(I heard this somewhere as a regular
Joke and put it to rhyme just for fun.)

Two guys are sharing a fifth of booze,
While gazing up at the sky
From the roof of a building in a large metropolis,
Forty stories high.

When one of 'em says to the other, "You know,
The wind up here is so strong,
It'll blow you right back if you fall off."
Says his pal, "You're flat out wrong."

"Nope," says the first, "I'll prove it to you."
And he steps off into space,
Falling away for a couple of stories,
Then rising back up to his place.

"You were just lucky," slurred the other.
"Bet you can't do it again."
So his friend once more staggers over to the edge
And leaps in the air with a grin.

And just as before, bobs up like a cork
Right back to the windblown roof.
"Well, I'll be danged," said his blurry-eyed friend.
"Twice in a row—that's proof."

Then taking one last swig from the bottle,
He launches out into space.
Down he plunges, but not like the other,
Goes splat all over the place!

Just then comes up another fellow
And stands by the first, looking down
At the ghastly scene in the street below,
Then speaks from behind a frown.

"We've been friends, you and me, forever.
But I'm tellin' you straight as I can,
You are one mean son-of-a-gun
When you're drinkin', Superman."

A Safecracker's Letter to Santa

(When Santa Believers Go Bad)

Santa, here's what I want for Christmas.
I hope you're paying attention.
A set of tools for padlock picking,
A crowbar, not to mention

A diamond drill for the big bank vaults,
Some dynamite and fuses,
A scaling ladder that telescopes,
And this year, no excuses.

I've asked you for all them things before,
But you ain't never come through.
You can't jimmy windows with a candy cane.
And a fruitcake just won't do.

Give me elevator shoes, a wig and the beard
I wrote you for last year,
And a new I.D. if things get hot
I'll need to disappear.

I've gone into kidnapping, and you might wanna know
Who it is I've snatched,
An angry old broad; she fought tooth and nail,
But key to the plan I've hatched.

I don't always operate legit, you know,
I'm unscrupulous and shady,
And if I don't get what I want this year,
It's curtains for your ol' lady.

Open Mic in Hell

(It's not against the law these days to write a poem in
rhyme and meter—but almost. I strike back with this
final piece.)

'Twas on a gloomy night in hell
The Devil said he'd like,

For culture's sake down in the pit,
To hold an open mic.

He sent his emissaries up
To wander to and fro

Upon the Earth and up and down
To where the poets go.

Invisible, the demons sat
And listened where they could

To poets' readings, and some did well
While others, not so good.

To every poet they whispered low,
As only the demons can do,

The offer to read at the open mic
Before the Devil's crew.

What an opportunity!
Thought many a bard, to go

Before his sulfurous majesty
And let their verses flow.

The audience would be numberless,
With souls all hell was jammed.

The living poets would all compete,
And the judges were the damned.

Now, all the souls in hell were men
(And some were women, too)

Who in their better moments past,
Remembered quite a few

Recitations from the works
Of poets they had read

When they were living or listened to
When they were tucked in bed.

And as the poets took their turns,
And as each line was told,

Some verses brought the damned to tears,
While others left them cold.

There was a verdict at the end,
According as they were moved

On those who failed to please the damned
And those whom they approved.

And after much deliberation
Amid the smoke and flame,

Down came the judgment and ever since,
Hell's not been the same.

All the rhyme and meter poets
Were let loose from the deep,

While all the modern free-verse dudes,
The Devil got to keep.